Wooden it be Cute!

51 Clever Designs Created with Wood Shapes

So much more than just cute shapes and characters, these fun projects to paint can frame your photos, keep track of notes, decorate a room, and hold your little treasures! Fashion them for the nursery, kid's rooms, and the kitchen. Celebrate the family pets with designs dedicated to your four-pawed pals. Decorate your porch and brighten your potted plants with garden-inspired signs and plant pokes. Best of all, the 51 projects are easy to paint and assemble from ready-made wood pieces. With these unique creations, you'll always have dozens of ideas for gifts!

Meggan Maravich designer

I live in Oklahoma with my husband, four young children, our Chihuahua, several barn cats and a few chickens. I began crafting by making Christmas gifts for our family the first year my husband and I were married. I enjoyed the experience so much, my hobby sort of snowballed and here I am today, thirteen years later. I've participated in craft shows and bazaars, volunteered to teach arts and crafts at school and church, been invited to share my designs with fellow crafters, painted signs and murals for local businesses, donated original artwork to charity, had many of my designs published in crafting magazines and … you're holding my first book!

My children keep me busy with our commute to school and their extra curricular activities (we have one ballerina, two karate black-belts, two beginner entomologists, three basketball players, four amateur scientists, four swimmers, four artists and a partridge in a pear tree). I manage to carve out some creative time for myself several times a week. Life is good!

I would love to thank some very important people for supporting my hobby over the years. Thank you, Grandma, for all the art supplies at Christmastime! Thank you, Dad and Mom, for your praise and encouragement. Thank you, Brady, Brannon, Amelia and Ayden, for your contagious enthusiasm for each and every project I design; and THANK YOU, Babe, for all your great ideas. I love you!

I also owe an expression of gratitude to my editors over the years, especially Annie Niemiec. Thank you, Annie, for the opportunity to share my love of crafting!

LEISURE ARTS, INC.
Little Rock, Arkansas

M000007066

general instructions

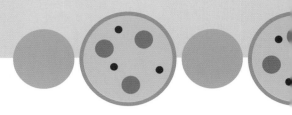

Assemble Forster® Woodsies® wood pieces with Delta Sobo® Glue and allow to dry before painting.

Sealing: I sealed all my wood surfaces prior to painting. (I did not seal the Woodsies® wood pieces). Use a wash brush or sponge brush to apply Delta Ceramcoat® All-Purpose Sealer evenly and allow to dry. Sand lightly and wipe clean with a dry cloth before painting. Painting raises the wood grain—sanding lightly between coats will ensure even coverage of your Delta Ceramcoat® acrylic paints.

Sanding: I use sanding blocks. I have a fine grit block to lightly sand across the top of a painted piece, and a coarse grit block to sand the edges of each piece. It is helpful to use an emery board for sanding the edges of the smaller pieces. Wipe with a clean, dry cloth before painting.
If you prefer a smooth finish without removing paint from the edges and corners, fold a brown paper lunch sack into a rectangle and sand with this.

Painting: For opaque coverage, basecoat all pieces with two coats of Delta Ceramcoat® Acrylic Paint.

Wash: For a stained look which allows the wood grain to show through, mix a wash with a 1:5 ratio of paint to water and wipe off excess paint with a dry cloth. Reapply wash to darken color. Sand and wipe clean.

Pattern Transfer: Copy the lettering or design onto tracing paper. Use a No. 2 pencil to rub over the lines on the back of the paper. Position the pattern onto the painted surface pencil side down. Go over the lines with a ballpoint pen. For a more permanent pattern (if you are making multiples of the same project), copy the lettering or design with a permanent marker onto tracing paper. Place the design over the painted surface and secure the top of the tracing paper with tape. Place a sheet of transfer paper between your pattern and the painted surface. Trace over the pattern with a stylus. I use a white eraser to remove the pattern lines once the paint has dried. It may be helpful to copy the patterns onto plain white paper and place a piece of waxed paper over the pattern. The pattern lines will show through, and you can glue the Woodsies® in place on top of the waxed paper and allow them to dry there.

Dry Brush: Some pieces have dry brushed edges; dab a small amount of paint onto a stencil brush and swirl the brush on a paper towel to remove as much paint as possible. Then run the dry brush across the edges of the piece, from front to back.

Shading and Highlighting: Use a flat brush. Dip one corner of the brush in water, the other in paint (lighter paint to highlight, darker paint to shade). Stroke the brush back and forth on the paper plate to blend; apply to the painted surface.

Sponging: Dip a natural sponge in water and squeeze out the excess. Dip the sponge in paint and dab the sponge on your piece. Add more paint to the sponge as needed.

Dip Dots: Use a stylus or the tip of a paintbrush handle. Dip into a small puddle of paint and dot onto your piece. Reload each time for same-sized dots. Experiment with different tools to determine which size best fits the project.

Eyes: I use the tip of a paintbrush to make large White dots. Place the dots close together, but don't overlap them. Allow to dry completely. Then use a smaller paintbrush handle or a stylus to dot the pupils Black. Practice on paper first to get a feel for how much paint and pressure to use and to judge the sizes of dots each tool makes.

Lettering: I transfer lettering to tracing paper so that I can center the word or words on the project. Go over the letters once, as if you were printing on paper, and then choose a paintbrush that will give you the desired thickness of the letters. For instance, a liner brush will give you uniform letters (pressing down gives a thicker line, letting up gives a thinner line). A flat brush will give your letters more dimension; I like flat brushes for script lettering.

Line Details: I use the Sakura Identi®-Pen dual-point black permanent marking pen to ink outline details on each painted piece to make them stand out. These are available online.

Gluing: Use a cool temp glue gun to attach finished pieces to your projects.

Helpful Tools: Needle nose pliers, wire snips, small tap hammer, scissors.

Embellishment Ideas: Fabric scraps, ribbon, rickrack, buttons, satin bows, colored craft thread.

Painting Surfaces and Forster® Woodsies®: Available at craft and hobby stores, or online.

Basic Instructions: Use Sobo® Glue to attach Woodsies® pieces when possible, and allow to dry. Paint the surface and pieces using several thin coats of paint rather than one thick coat. Allow to dry thoroughly. Sand smooth between coats; sand heavily and remove paint from the edges after painting is complete. Attach the pieces to the surface using a cool temp glue gun. Ink the outline details with a black marking pen. Finish the project with embellishments and hardware for hanging.

puppy welcome

Surface
Forster® Woodsies®
7¼" x 2¹³/₁₆" x ¼" Wood Slat

Wood Pieces
(2) Small Octagons (paws)
(1) Large Oval (head),
(2) Small Ovals (ears)

Other Supplies
(2) Small Screw Eyes, Needle
Nose Pliers, 18" Fabric Strip, 6"
Coordinating Fabric Strip

**Delta Ceramcoat® Acrylic
Paints**
Timberline Green
White
Espresso
Black

INSTRUCTIONS
1. Attach the ears to the back of the head with Sobo® Glue.
2. Paint as follows:
Wood Slat – Timberline Green
Lettering – White
Paws, Head, and Ears – White with Espresso spots
Eyes – Black dip dots
Nose – Black
3. Sand the pieces and wipe clean.
4. Attach the paws to the front of the slat and the head and ears behind the slat.
5. Ink the outline details with the black marking pen.
6. Finish – Press and twist the screw eyes into the top corners of the sign. Use the pliers to tighten. Thread the long fabric strip through the screw eyes; knot the fabric ends. Knot the short fabric strip to the center of the hanger. Trim the fabric ends.

puppy ornament

Surface
3½" x 4½" x ⅛" Wood Rectangle
(Lara's Crafts)
Wood Pieces
(1) XXL Teardrop (body)
(1) Medium Teardrop (tail)
(2) Medium Ovals (ears)
Other Supplies
Small Screw Eye, Needle Nose Pliers,
Fabric Strip for Rag Bow, Wire Ornament
Hook
Delta Ceramcoat® Acrylic Paints
Timberline Green
Latte
Espresso
Black

INSTRUCTIONS
1. Assemble the puppy using Sobo® Glue.
2. Paint as follows:
Wood Rectangle – Timberline Green
Puppy – Latte with Espresso spots;
   dry brush edges Espresso
Eyes – Black dip dots
Nose – Black
3. Sand the pieces and wipe clean.
4. Ink the outline details with the black
   marking pen.
5. Attach the puppy to the ornament using
   a cool temp glue gun.
6. Finish – Press and twist the screw eye
   into the top center of the ornament. Use
   the pliers to tighten. Use the pliers to
   bend the ornament hook into a curly
   backwards "S." Loop the ornament hook
   through the screw eye. Knot the center
   of the fabric strip to form a rag bow.
   Attach the rag bow over the screw eye
   with a cool temp glue gun. Trim the
   fabric ends.

puppy peg rack

Surface
1½" x 11⅞" Wood Peg Rack

Wood Pieces
Puppy A
(1) Large Rectangle (body)
(1) Medium Oval (head)
(5) Small Ovals (feet, ear)
(1) Small Teardrop (tail)
Puppy B
(1) XL Teardrop (body)
(1) Medium Teardrop (tail)
(2) Medium Ovals (ears)

Other Supplies
Sawtooth Hanger

Delta Ceramcoat® Acrylic Paints
Timberline Green
Golden Brown
Latte
Espresso
Black

INSTRUCTIONS
1. Assemble the puppies using Sobo® Glue.
2. Paint as follows:
Peg Rack – Timberline Green
Puppy A – Golden Brown with Espresso spots; dry brush edges with Espresso
Puppy B – Latte with Espresso spots; dry brush edges with Espresso
Eyes – Black dip dots
Noses – Black
3. Sand the pieces and wipe clean.
4. Ink the outline details with the black marking pen.
5. Finish – Attach the puppies to the front of the peg rack using a cool temp glue gun. Attach the sawtooth hanger to the back of the peg rack.

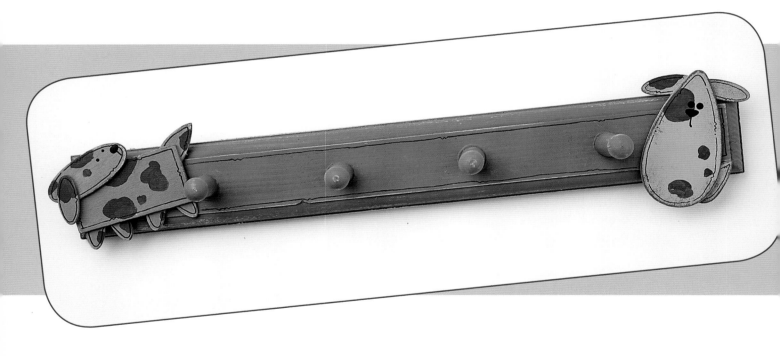

puppy treats tag

Surface
2³/₄" x 5¹/₄" Wood Tag (Lara's Crafts),
Glass Jar with Lid

Wood Pieces
(2) Large Rectangles (body, sign)
(1) Small Teardrop (tail)
(5) Small Ovals (feet, ear)
(1) Medium Oval (head)

Other Supplies
Fabric Strip

Delta Ceramcoat® Acrylic Paints
Timberline Green
White
Espresso
Latte
Spice Brown
Black

INSTRUCTIONS
1. Assemble the puppy using Sobo® Glue.
2. Paint as follows:
Tag – Timberline Green
Puppy – White with Espresso spots
Eyes – Black dip dots
Nose – Black
Sign – Spice Brown
Lettering – Latte
3. Sand the pieces and wipe clean.
4. Ink the outline details with the black
   marking pen.
5. Finish – Attach the pieces to the tag using a cool
   temp glue gun. Thread the fabric strip through
   the tag and around the jar. Knot and trim the
   fabric ends.

7

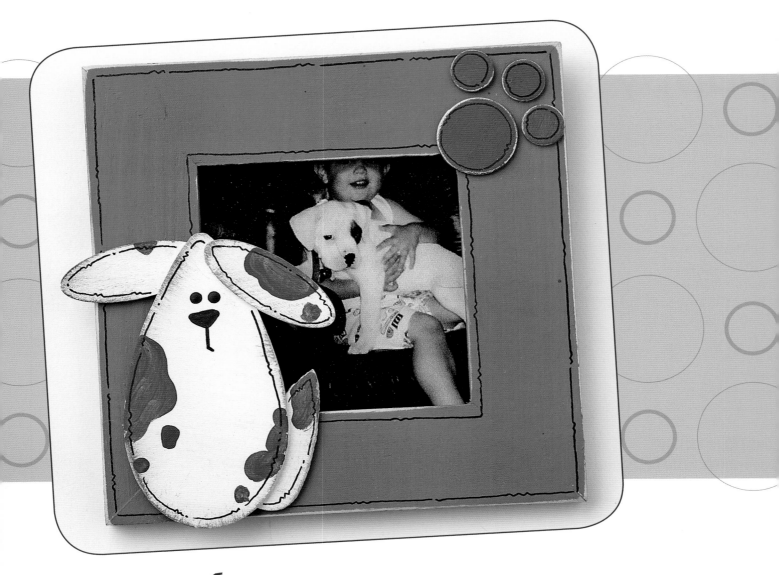

puppy frame

Surface
5" x 5" Wood Photo Frame
Wood Pieces
(1) XXL Teardrop (body)
(1) Medium Teardrop (tail)
(2) Medium Ovals (ears)
(3) Small Circles (paw print)
(1) Medium Circle (paw print)
Delta Ceramcoat® Acrylic Paints
Timberline Green
White
Espresso
Spice Brown
Black

INSTRUCTIONS
1. Assemble the puppy using Sobo® Glue.
2. Paint as follows:
Frame – Timberline Green
Puppy – White with Espresso spots; dry brush edges Espresso
Paw Print – Spice Brown
Eyes – Black dip dots
Nose – Black
3. Sand the pieces and wipe clean.
4. Ink the outline details with the black marking pen.
5. Finish – Attach the pieces to the front of the frame using a cool temp glue gun.

kitty welcome

Surface
Forster® Woodsies®
7¼" x 2¹³/₁₆" x ¼" Wood Slat

Wood Pieces
(1) Large Oval (head)
(1) Medium Triangle (ears)
(2) Medium Circles (paws)

Other Supplies
(2) Small Screw Eyes, Needle
Nose Pliers, 18" Fabric Strip,
6" Coordinating Fabric Strip

**Delta Ceramcoat® Acrylic
Paints**
Barn Red
White
Black
Espresso

INSTRUCTIONS

1. Attach the ears to the back of the head with Sobo® Glue.
2. Paint as follows:
   Wood Slat – Barn Red
   Lettering – White
   Head, Ears, and Paws – White; dry brush edges Espresso
   Eyes – Black dip dots
   Nose – Black
3. Sand the pieces and wipe clean.
4. Attach the paws to the front of the slat and the head and the ears behind the slat using a cool temp glue gun.
5. Ink the outline details with the black marking pen.
6. Finish – Press and twist the screw eyes into the top corners of the sign. Use the pliers to tighten. Thread the long fabric strip through the screw eyes; knot the fabric ends. Knot the short fabric strip to the center of the hanger. Trim the fabric ends.

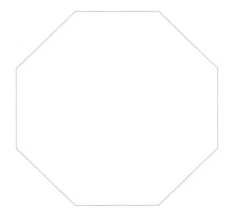

kitty
ornament

Surface
3¹/₂" x 4¹/₂" x ¹/₈" Wood Rectangle
(Lara's Crafts)
Wood Pieces
(1) XXL Oval (body)
(2) Medium Teardrops (ears)
Other Supplies
Small Screw Eye, Needle Nose
Pliers, Fabric Strip for rag bow, Wire
Ornament Hook
Delta Ceramcoat® Acrylic Paints
Barn Red
Drizzle Grey
Black

INSTRUCTIONS:
1. Assemble the kitty with Sobo® Glue.
2. Paint as follows:
Wood Rectangle – Barn Red
Kitty – Drizzle Grey with Black stripes
Eyes – Black dip dots
Nose – Black
3. Sand the pieces and wipe clean.
4. Ink the outline details with the black marking pen.
5. Attach the kitty to the ornament using a cool temp glue gun.
6. Finish – Press and twist the screw eye into the top center of the ornament. Use the pliers to tighten. Use the pliers to bend the ornament hook into a curly backwards "S." Loop the ornament hook through the screw eye. Knot the center of the fabric strip to form a rag bow. Attach the rag bow over the screw eye with a cool temp glue gun. Trim the fabric ends.

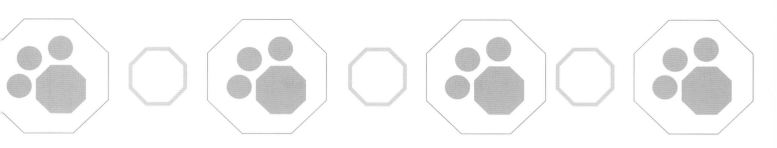

kitty peg rack

Surface
1 1/2" x 11 7/8" Wood Peg Rack

Wood Pieces
Kitty A
(1) Large Oval (body)
(2) Small Teardrops (ears)
Kitty B
(1) Medium Oval (body)
(1) Small Octagon (head)
(5) Small Ovals (feet, tail)
(1) Small Triangle (ears)

Other Supplies
Sawtooth Hanger

Delta Ceramcoat® Acrylic Paints
Barn Red
Drizzle Grey
White
Espresso
Black

INSTRUCTIONS
1. Assemble the kitties with Sobo® Glue.
2. Paint as follows:
Peg Rack – Barn Red
Kitty A – White with Espresso stripes; dry brush edges Espresso

Kitty B – Drizzle Grey with Black stripes
Eyes – Black dip dots
Noses – Black
3. Sand the pieces and wipe clean.
4. Ink the outline details with the black marking pen.
5. Finish – Attach the kitties to the front of the peg rack using a cool temp glue gun. Attach a sawtooth hanger to the back of the peg rack.

kitty treats tag

Surface
4³/₈" x 2¹/₄" Wood Tag (Lara's Crafts),
Glass Jar with Lid
Wood Pieces
(1) Medium Rectangle (sign)
(1) Large Oval (body)
(5) Small Ovals (feet, tail)
(1) Small Octagon (head)
(1) Small Triangle (ears)
Other Supplies
Fabric Strip
Delta Ceramcoat® Acrylic Paints
Barn Red
Golden Brown
Espresso
Latte
Black

INSTRUCTIONS
1. Assemble the kitty with Sobo® Glue.
2. Paint as follows:
Tag – Barn Red
Kitty – Golden Brown with Espresso stripes
Eyes – Black dip dots
Nose – Black
Sign – Espresso
Lettering – Latte
3. Sand the pieces and wipe clean.
4. Ink the outline details with the black marking pen.
5. Finish – Attach the pieces to the tag using a cool temp glue gun. Thread the fabric strip through the tag and around the jar. Knot and trim the fabric ends.

kitty frame

Surface
5" x 5" Wood Photo Frame
Wood Pieces
(1) XXL Oval (body)
(2) Medium Teardrops (ears)
(1) Small Octagon (paw print)
(3) Small Circles (paw print)
Delta Ceramcoat® Acrylic Paints
Barn Red
Golden Brown
Espresso
Spice Brown
Black

INSTRUCTIONS
1. Assemble the kitty with Sobo® Glue.
2. Paint as follows:
Frame – Barn Red
Kitty – Golden Brown with Espresso stripes
Paw Print – Spice Brown
Eyes – Black dip dots
Nose – Black
3. Sand the pieces and wipe clean.

4. Ink the outline details with the black marking pen.
5. Finish – Attach the pieces to the front of the frame using a cool temp glue gun.

13

saltbox house plaque

Surface
5¹/₄" x 7¹/₄" Wood Plaque
(Walnut Hollow)
Wood Pieces
(2) Medium Ovals (tree tops)
(1) Large Square (house)
(5) Small Squares (chimneys & sheep)
(5) Small Triangles (roof)
Other Supplies
(2) Small Screw Eyes, Needle Nose Pliers, 18" Fabric Strip
Delta Ceramcoat® Acrylic Paints
Spa Blue
Light Foliage Green
Medium Foliage Green
Green Tea
Barn Red
Black
White
Espresso

INSTRUCTIONS
1. Paint as follows:
Sky and Plaque Edges –
    Spa Blue
Hills and Tree Tops –
    Light Foliage Green
Shade Hills and Tree
    Tops – Medium Foliage
    Green
Highlight Hills and Tree Tops –
    Green Tea
Tree Trunks – Espresso
House and Chimneys –
    Barn Red; dry brush edges
    Espresso
Roof, Windows and Door –
    Black
Sheep and Sheep Tails – White
Sheep Heads, Ears and Feet –
    Black
2. Sand the pieces and wipe clean.
3. Ink the outline details with the black marking pen.
4. Attach the pieces to the plaque using a cool temp glue gun.
5. Finish – Press and twist the screw eyes into the top of the sign. Use the pliers to tighten. Thread the fabric strip through the screw eyes; knot the fabric ends. Trim the fabric ends.

saltbox house door hanger

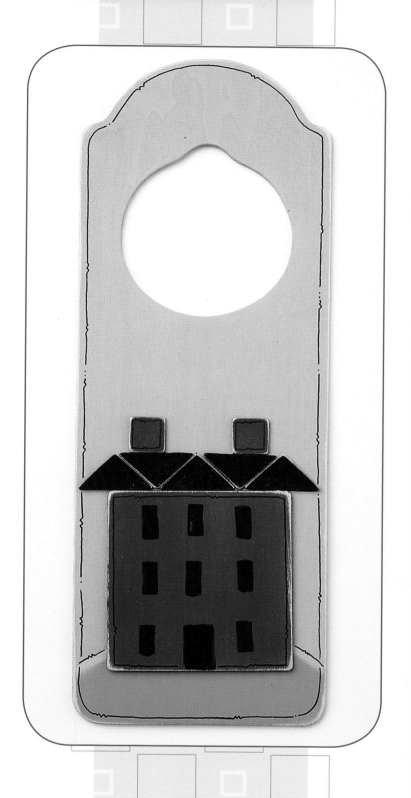

Surface
3¹/₂" x 9¹/₂" Adoorable Hanger with Arch
(Lara's Crafts)
Wood Pieces
(1) Large Square (house)
(2) Small Squares (chimneys)
(5) Small Triangles (roof)
Delta Ceramcoat® Acrylic Paints
Spa Blue
Light Foliage Green
Green Tea
Barn Red
Black

INSTRUCTIONS
1. Paint as follows:
Door Hanger – Spa Blue
Hill – Light Foliage Green
Highlight Hill – Green Tea
House and Chimneys – Barn Red
Roof, Windows and Door – Black
2. Sand the pieces and wipe clean.
3. Ink the outline details with the black
   marking pen.
4. Finish – Attach the pieces to the door
   hanger using a cool temp glue gun.

pineapple welcome sign

Surface
7" x 9" Wood Oval Plaque (Walnut Hollow)

Wood Pieces
(1) XL Teardrop (pineapple)
(1) Medium Star (base)
(1) Large Star (leaves)
(1) XL Star (leaves)
(2) Small Teardrops (accents)
(2) Medium Teardrops (accents)

Other Supplies
Sawtooth Hanger

Delta Ceramcoat® Acrylic Paints
Green Tea
Golden Brown
Espresso
Timberline Green
Butter Yellow

INSTRUCTIONS
1. Assemble the pineapple with Sobo® Glue.
2. Attach a sawtooth hanger onto the back of the plaque.
3. Paint as follows:
Plaque – Green Tea
Pineapple – Golden Brown; dry brush edges Espresso
Details on Pineapple – Espresso
Leaves, Base, and Word – Timberline Green
Accents – Butter Yellow
4. Sand the pieces and wipe clean.
5. Ink the outline details with the black marking pen.
6. Finish – Attach the pieces to the sign using a cool temp glue gun.

welcome to our pad

Surface
14" x 6" Innkeeper Signboard
(Walnut Hollow)
Wood Pieces
(2) Large Ovals (frog bodies)
(2) Large Hearts (frog legs)
(4) Small Stars (frog feet)
(4) Small Circles (frog eyes)
(6) Small Ovals (cattails)
Alphabet Tiles
(1) Each W, L, C, M, T, U, R, P,
A, D; (2) E; (3) O
Other Supplies
Sawtooth Hanger
Delta Ceramcoat® Acrylic Paints
Gecko
Medium Foliage Green
Light Foliage Green
Green Tea

Black
White
Spice Brown

INSTRUCTIONS
1. Assemble the frogs with Sobo® Glue.
2. Attach a sawtooth hanger onto the back of the sign.
3. Paint as follows:
Sign – Gecko
Frog A – Light Foliage Green with Medium Foliage Green and Green Tea dip dots
Frog B – Medium Foliage Green with Light Foliage Green and Green Tea dip dots
Eyes – Large White dip dots with smaller Black dip dot centers

Cattails – Spice Brown
Cattail Leaves – Strokes of Medium Foliage Green and Light Foliage Green
Alphabet Tiles – Medium Foliage Green Wash
4. Sand the pieces and wipe clean.
5. Ink the outline details with the black marking pen.
6. Finish – Attach the pieces to the sign using a cool temp glue gun.

frog plant poke

For each plant poke, you will need:
Surface
2" x 3" Rectangle Sign (Lara's Crafts),
Jumbo Craft Stick
Wood Pieces
(1) Large Oval (frog body)
(1) Large Heart (frog legs)
(2) Small Stars (frog feet)
(2) Small Circles (frog eyes)
Other Supplies
6" Fabric Strip
Delta Ceramcoat® Acrylic Paints
Gecko
Medium Foliage Green
Light Foliage Green
Green Tea
Black
White
Green

INSTRUCTIONS
1. Assemble each frog with Sobo® Glue.
2. Paint as follows:
Rectangle – Gecko
Jumbo Craft Stick – Green wash
Frog A – Medium Foliage Green with Light
   Foliage Green and Green Tea dip dots
Frog B – Light Foliage Green with Medium
   Foliage Green and Green Tea dip dots
Eyes – Large White dip dots with smaller
   Black dip dot centers
3. Sand the pieces and wipe clean.
4. Ink the outline details with the black
   marking pen.
5. Finish – Attach the craft stick to the
   back of the rectangle and the frog to the
   front using a cool temp glue gun. Knot
   the center of the fabric strip to form a
   rag bow. Attach the rag bow to the plant
   poke with a cool temp glue gun. Trim
   the fabric ends.

frog magnets

For each magnet, you will need:

Wood Pieces
(1) Large Oval (frog body)
(1) XL Heart (frog legs)
(2) Small Stars (frog feet)
(2) Small Circles (frog eyes)

Other Supplies
Round Button Magnet

Delta Ceramcoat® Acrylic Paints
Light Foliage Green
Medium Foliage Green
Dark Foliage Green
Black
White

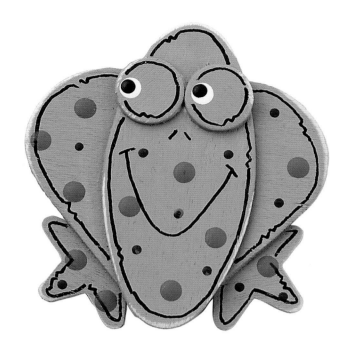

INSTRUCTIONS

1. Assemble the frog with Sobo® Glue.
2. Paint as follows:

Frog A – Light Foliage Green with Medium
    Foliage Green and Dark Foliage Green dip dots

Frog B – Medium Foliage Green with Light
    Foliage Green and Dark Foliage Green dip dots

Eyes – Large White dip dots with smaller Black
    dip dot centers

3. Sand the pieces and wipe clean.
4. Ink the outline details with the black
    marking pen.
5. Finish – Attach the button magnet to the
    back of the frog body.

 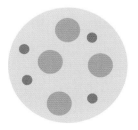  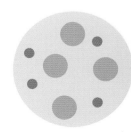

garden welcome

Surface

14" x 6" Innkeeper Signboard (Walnut Hollow)

Wood Pieces

(4) Small Hearts (butterfly wings)
(18) Small Teardrops (butterfly wings and daisy petals)
(8) Small Ovals (butterfly bodies and dragonfly wings and body)
(3) Small Octagons (daisy centers)

Other Supplies

(2) Small Screw Eyes, Needle Nose Pliers, Wire Snips,
(2) 6" Fabric Strips, 16" Craft Wire

Delta Ceramcoat® Medium

Sparkle Glaze

Delta Ceramcoat® Acrylic Paints

Hope
Gecko
White
Laguna Blue
Citrus
Black

INSTRUCTIONS

1. Assemble the daisies, butterflies and dragonfly with Sobo® Glue.
2. Paint as follows:
Sign – Hope
Butterfly A – Citrus
Butterfly B – Gecko
Dragonfly – Laguna Blue
Eyes – Large White dip dots with smaller Black dip dot centers
Daisies – White with Citrus centers

Lettering – Black
3. Sand the pieces and wipe clean.
4. Ink the outline details with the black marking pen.
5. Finish – Attach the pieces to the sign using a cool temp glue gun. Press and twist the screw eyes into the top corners of the sign. Use the pliers to tighten. Curl the craft wire around a paintbrush handle, thread through the screw eyes and twist the ends to secure. Knot the fabric scraps to create rag bows. Trim the fabric ends. Attach bows with a cool temp glue gun. Brush Sparkle Glaze onto the insect wings.

butterfly plant pokes

Surface
(2) Jumbo Craft Sticks
Wood Pieces
Large Butterfly
(1) Large Oval (body)
(2) Large Teardrops (wings)
(2) Large Hearts (wings)
Small Butterfly
(1) Medium Oval (body)
(2) Medium Teardrops (wings)
(2) Medium Hearts (wings)
Delta Ceramcoat® Medium
Sparkle Glaze
Delta Ceramcoat® Acrylic Paints
Hope
Black
OJ
Sweet Pea
Gecko
Pop Pink

INSTRUCTIONS
1. Assemble the butterflies with Sobo® Glue.
2. Paint as follows:
Jumbo Craft Sticks – Hope
Large Butterfly: Pop Pink (body), Sweet Pea and
    Gecko (wings) with Pop Pink and OJ dip dot
    wing details
Small Butterfly: OJ (body), Gecko and
    Sweet Pea (wings) with Pop Pink and OJ dip
    dot wing details
Eyes – small Black dip dots
3. Sand the pieces and wipe clean.
4. Ink the outline details with the black
    marking pen.
5. Finish – Attach the butterfies to the craft stick
    using a cool temp glue gun. Brush Sparkle
    Glaze onto the wings.

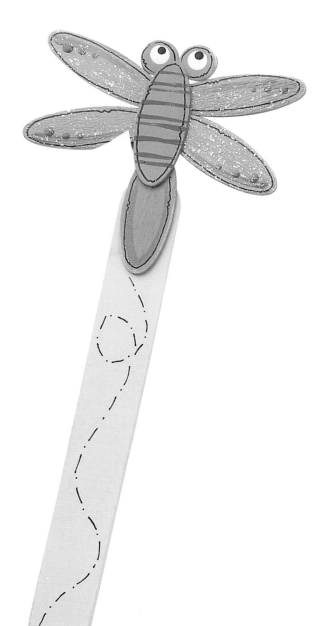

dragonfly plant poke

Surface
Jumbo Craft Stick
Wood Pieces
(6) Medium Ovals (wings and body)
(2) Small Circles (eyes)
Delta Ceramcoat® Medium
Sparkle Glaze
Delta Ceramcoat® Acrylic Paints
Hope
Tahiti Blue
Mediterranean
Laguna Blue
White
Black

INSTRUCTIONS
1. Assemble the Dragonfly with Sobo® Glue.
2. Paint as follows:
Jumbo Craft Stick – Hope
Dragonfly – Tahiti Blue with Mediterranean and Laguna Blue details
Eyes – large White dip dots with smaller Black dip dot centers
3. Sand the pieces and wipe clean.
4. Ink the outline details with the black marking pen.
5. Finish – Attach the dragonfly to the craft stick using a cool temp glue gun. Brush Sparkle Glaze onto the wings.

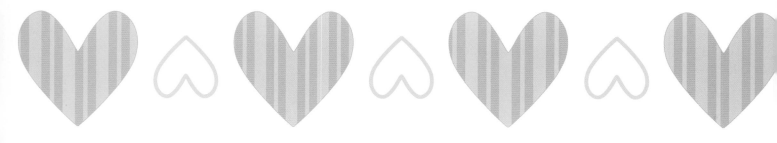

daisy frame

Surface
5" x 5" Wood Photo Frame
Wood Pieces
(3) Medium Octagons
(14) Small Ovals
Delta Ceramcoat® Medium
Sparkle Glaze
Delta Ceramcoat® Acrylic Paints
Light Foliage Green
Enchanted
Gecko
White
Citrus

INSTRUCTIONS
1. Assemble the daisies with Sobo® Glue.
2. Paint as follows:
Bottom of the Frame – Light Foliage Green
Checks and Dip Dots – Gecko
Top of the Frame – Enchanted
Daisy Petals – White
Daisy Centers – Citrus
3. Sand the pieces and wipe clean.

4. Attach the daisies to the frame using a cool temp glue gun.
5. Finish – Ink the outline details with the black marking pen. Apply Sparkle Glaze to the daisies.

daisy hinged box

Surface
8 1/8"w x 6 5/8"h x 4 1/4"d Wood Hinged Storage Box
Wood Pieces
(9) Medium Octagons
(42) Small Ovals
(2) Medium Teardrops
(1) Small Teardrop
Delta Ceramcoat® Medium Sparkle Glaze
Delta Ceramcoat® Acrylic Paints

Light Foliage Green
Enchanted
Gecko
White
Citrus

INSTRUCTIONS
1. Assemble the daisies with Sobo® Glue.
2. Paint as follows:
Leaves and Bottom of Box – Light Foliage Green

Checks and Dip Dots – Gecko
Top of Box – Enchanted
Daisy Petals – White
Daisy Centers – Citrus
3. Sand the pieces and wipe clean.
4. Attach the daisies to the box using a cool temp glue gun.
5. Ink the outline details with the black marking pen.
6. Finish – Apply Sparkle Glaze to the daisies.

24

TOP

LEFT SIDE   **RIGHT SIDE**

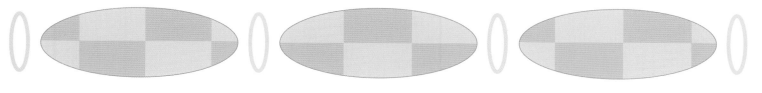

25

daisy door hanger

Surface
3¹/₂" x 9¹/₂" Adoorable Hanger with Arch (Lara's Crafts)
Wood Pieces
(3) Medium Octagons
(14) Small Ovals
Delta Ceramcoat® Medium
Sparkle Glaze
Delta Ceramcoat® Acrylic Paints
Light Foliage Green
Enchanted
Gecko
White
Citrus

INSTRUCTIONS:
1. Assemble the Daisies with Sobo® Glue.
2. Paint as follows:
Bottom of Door Hanger – Light Foliage Green
Checks and Dip Dots – Gecko
Top of Door Hanger – Enchanted
Daisy Petals – White
Daisy Centers – Citrus
3. Sand the pieces and wipe clean.
4. Attach the daisies to the door hanger using a cool temp glue gun.
5. Ink the outline details with the black marking pen.
6. Finish – Apply Sparkle Glaze to the daisies.

animal trio sign

Surface
10" x 3³/₈" x ¹/₈" Rectangle Sign (Lara's Crafts)

Wood Pieces

Bunny
(1) XL Circle (head)
(2) L Teardrops (ears)
(2) Medium Circles (muzzle)
(1) Small Circle (nose)

Bear
(1) XL Circle (head)
(1) Large Circle (muzzle)
(2) Medium Circles (ears)
(1) Small Circle (nose)

Mouse
(1) XL Circle (head)
(2) Large Circles (ears)
(1) Small Circle (nose)

Other Supplies
12" Craft Wire for hanging, Wire Snips, 9" Ribbon, 3" Pink Twill Tape for bow

Delta Ceramcoat® Acrylic Paints
Moroccan Red
Latte
Think Pink
Fleshtone
Espresso
Black
Drizzle Grey
White

INSTRUCTIONS

1. Assemble the animals with Sobo® Glue.
2. Paint as follows:
Sign – Moroccan Red
Bunny: Latte (head and ears); Fleshtone (muzzle); Latte (dip dots on muzzle); Think Pink (insides of ears and nose)
Bear: Espresso (head and ears); Latte (muzzle); Black (dip dots on muzzle); Black (nose)
Mouse: Drizzle Grey (head and ears); Think Pink (insides of ears and nose)
All Eyes – large White dip dots with smaller Black dip dot centers
3. Sand the pieces and wipe clean.
4. Ink the dashed outline stitches and the details with the black marking pen.
5. Finish – Knot the twill tape to create a bow; trim the ends. Attach the animals to the sign and the bow under the bear's chin using a cool temp glue gun. Curl the craft wire around a paintbrush handle, thread through the holes and twist the ends to secure. Tie a ribbon bow around the wire; trim the ends.

toy zone sign

Surface
9" x 12" Wood Plaque (Walnut Hollow)

Wood Pieces

Jack-in-the-Box
(1) XL Square
(1) XL Star
(1) Mini Craft Stick (Spring)
(1) Large Triangle (Shirt)
(2) Small Stars (Hat & Collar)
(2) Small Teardrops (Arms)
(1) Medium Oval (Head)
(1) Small Circle (Nose)

Truck
(1) Large Square (Cab)
(1) XL Square (Trailer)
(1) Medium Rectangle (Grill)
(2) Small Circles (Headlights)
(2) Mini Craft Sticks (Wheels)

Elephant
(1) Large Circle (head)
(1) XL Circle (body)
(1) Small Oval (nose)
(2) Small Hearts (ears)
(4) Small Rectangles (feet)

Ball
(1) XXL Circle

Blocks
(4) Small Squares
(2) Small Rectangles
(1) Large Triangle

Letters
(4) 2" Wood Squares
¼" thick Wood Alpha Cutouts
"T – O – Y – S"

Other Supplies
Sawtooth Hanger, (2) 3" Lengths Craft Thread, Pink Powder Blush

Delta Ceramcoat® Acrylic Paints
Moroccan Red
Black
Fleshtone
Gecko
Blue Heaven
Blissful Blue
Butter Yellow
White
Opaque Blue
Citrus
OJ

INSTRUCTIONS
1. Assemble the Jack-in-the-Box, Truck, and Elephant, with Sobo® Glue.
2. Attach a sawtooth hanger to the back of the plaque.
3. Paint as follows:

Plaque – Moroccan Red

Jack in the Box – Box Gecko. Star and Spring Blue Heaven. Shirt and Sleeves OJ with Blue Heaven dip dots. Head and Arms Fleshtone. Hat and Collar Gecko. Nose Moroccan Red. Blush cheeks with Pink Powder Blush. Eyes are Black dip dots.

Truck – Cab and Trailer Butter Yellow; grill Blissful Blue; headlights White; wheels Black.

Elephant – Body, Ears, and Feet Blue Heaven with OJ dots. Head and Trunk Blue Heaven. Blush cheeks with pink powder blush. Eyes are Black dip dots.

Ball – White. Sections are Moroccan Red, Opaque Blue and Butter Yellow.

Blocks – (2) Squares Butter Yellow, (1) Square Opaque Blue, (1) Square OJ. Rectangles Opaque Blue and OJ. Triangle Opaque Blue.

Letter Squares – one each OJ, Blue Heaven, Gecko, Citrus

T – Citrus
O – OJ
Y – Blue Heaven
S – Gecko

4. Sand the pieces and wipe clean.
5. Ink the outline details with the black marking pen.
6. Finish – Attach the toys to the front of the plaque using a cool temp glue gun. Attach the letters to the squares, then the squares to the front of the plaque with a cool temp glue gun. Tie the craft thread into a bow and glue to the elephant's neck.

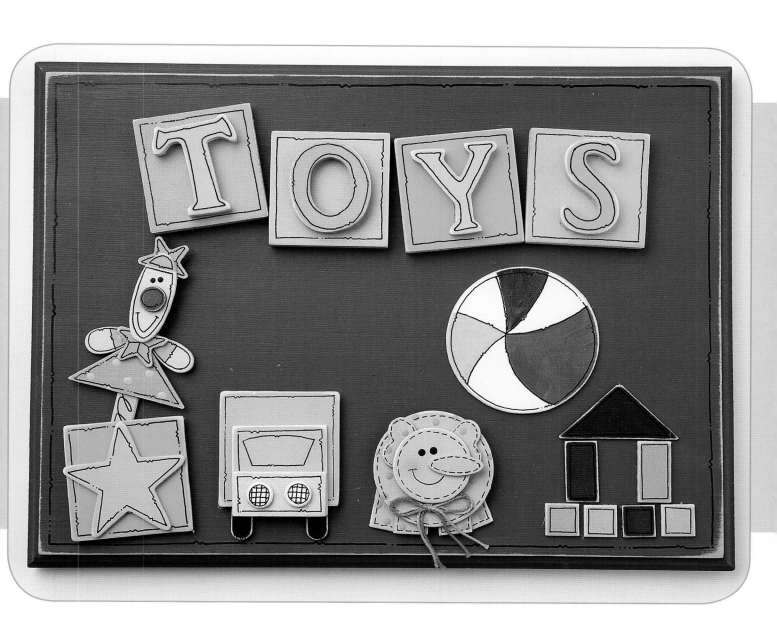

treasure map wall art

Surface
24" x 36" Stretched Canvas
Wood Pieces
Pirate Ship
(1) Small Rectangle (sail)
(1) Medium Rectangle (sail)
(1) Large Rectangle (sail)
(1) Small Triangle (flag)
Compass
(1) Large Circle
(1) XL Circle
(1) XXL Circle
(4) Medium Teardrops
Large Palm Tree
(2) Small Triangles (trunk)
(2) Medium Triangles (trunk)
(1) Large Triangle (trunk)
(1) Medium Heart (leaves)
(4) Medium Teardrops (leaves)
(1) Small Teardrop (leaves)
(3) Small Circles (coconuts)
Small Palm Tree
(3) Small Triangles (trunk)
(3) Medium Triangles (trunk)
(1) Small Heart (leaves)
(3) Small Teardrops (leaves)
(1) Small Circle (coconut)
Treasure Chest
(2) Large Rectangles
Delta Ceramcoat® Medium
Sparkle Glaze

Delta Ceramcoat® Acrylic Paints
Opaque Blue
Latte
Espresso
Black
Light Foliage Green
Medium Foliage Green
Golden Brown
Citrus
Opaque Red
Green
Blissful Blue
Mediterranean
Spa Blue
Butter Yellow
Timberline Green

INSTRUCTIONS:
1. Transfer the map outline onto the canvas.
2. Assemble the Palm Trees and Compass with Sobo® Glue.
3. Paint as follows:
Map – Latte; shade with Espresso
Edges of Canvas – Opaque Blue
Shade Behind Map – Black
4. Transfer the map details.
5. Paint as follows:
Land Masses – Light Foliage Green; shade with Medium Foliage Green; outline with Espresso
Waves under Pirate Ship – Spa Blue
Pirate Ship, Treasure Chest, Palm Trees, Words, and Coconuts – Golden Brown; shade with Espresso
N,E,S,W and dashes around map edges – Espresso
Palm Leaves – Timberline Green
Coins – dip dots of Citrus
Jewels – dip dots of Opaque Red and Green
Sails – Blissful Blue; shade with Mediterranean
Flag and treasure trail – Opaque Red
Compass circles from top to bottom – Butter Yellow, Spa Blue and Opaque Red
Compass Needles – Opaque Red
6. Sand the pieces and wipe clean.
7. Ink the outline details with the black marking pen.
8. Finish – Attach the pieces to the canvas using a cool temp glue gun. Brush Sparkle Glaze over coins and jewels.

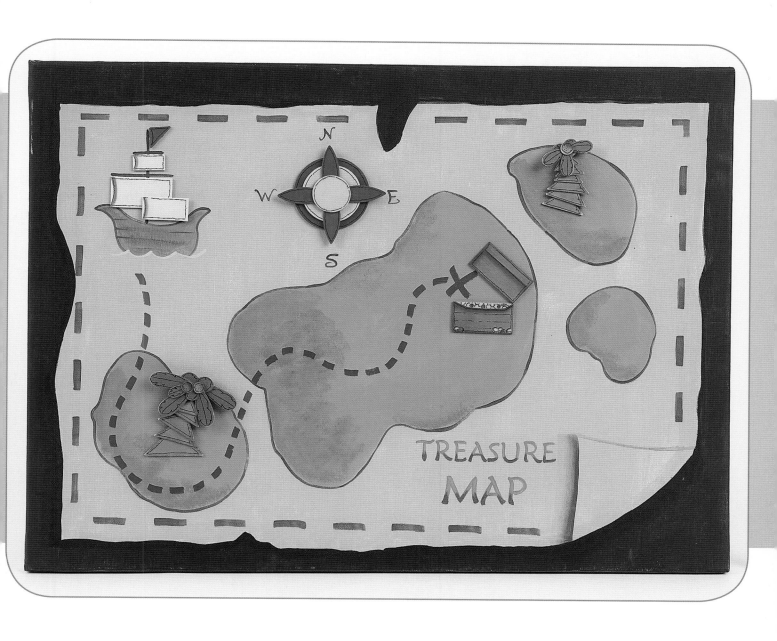

pirate frame

Surface
5" x 5" Wood Photo Frame
Wood Pieces
(1) Medium Circle (head)
(1) Medium Square (shirt)
(1) Small Triangle (sleeve)
(2) Small Ovals (arm, parrot)
Delta Ceramcoat® Acrylic Paints
Latte
Espresso
Fleshtone
Moroccan Red
Black
White
Butter Yellow
Green

INSTRUCTIONS

1. Paint as follows:
Frame – Latte
Dashes – Espresso
Pirate Arm and Head –
   Fleshtone
Bandanna – Moroccan Red
Eye and Eye Patch – Black
Shirt and Sleeve – White with
   Moroccan Red stripes
Parrot – Green with Butter
   Yellow eyes and beak
2. Sand the pieces and wipe
   clean.
3. Ink the outline details with
   the black marking pen.
4. Finish – Attach the pieces to
   the frame using a cool temp
   glue gun.

bug frame

Surface
5" x 5" Wood Photo Frame

Wood Pieces
(2) Small Rectangles
(6) Small Circles
(1) Small Triangle
(1) Large Square
(2) Small Ovals
(1) Medium Oval
(1) Large Oval

Delta Ceramcoat® Medium
Sparkle Glaze

Delta Ceramcoat® Acrylic Paints
Tahiti Blue
White
Black
Green
Gecko
Citrus
OJ

INSTRUCTIONS
1. Assemble the bugs with Sobo® Glue.
2. Paint as follows:
Frame – Tahiti Blue
Bug A – (1) Small Rectangle – OJ with Citrus dots
Bug B – (1) Small Rectangle and (2) Small Circles – Citrus
   (1) Small Triangle – Gecko
   (1) Large Square – OJ with Gecko dip dots
Bug C – (1) Medium Oval Green with OJ stripes
   (2) Small Circles – Green
   (1) Small Oval – Gecko
Bug D – (1) Small Oval Citrus with Gecko dip dots
Bug E – (1) Large Oval Gecko and OJ with Green dip dots
   (2) Small Circles OJ
Eyes are White with Black dip dots
Legs – Black
3. Sand the pieces lightly and wipe clean.
4. Ink the outline details with the black marking pen.
5. Finish – Attach the bugs to the frame using a cool temp glue gun. Brush Sparkle Glaze over the bug bodies.

bug box

Surface
3³/₄"w x 2¹/₈"h x 2⁷/₈"d Small
Hinged Box

Wood Pieces
(1) Large Oval
(2) Small Circles
(1) Small Rectangle
(2) Small Squares

Delta Ceramcoat® Medium
Sparkle Glaze

Delta Ceramcoat® Acrylic Paints
Tahiti Blue
White
Black
Green
Gecko
Citrus
OJ

INSTRUCTIONS

1. Assemble Large Bug with Sobo® Glue.
2. Paint as follows:
Box – Tahiti Blue
Large Bug – (1) Large Oval OJ and Gecko with Green dip dots
   (2) Small Circles Gecko
Small Bug A – (1) Small Square Gecko with Citrus dip dots
Small Bug B – (1) Small Square Citrus with Green dip dots
Small Bug C – (1) Small Rectangle Gecko with Green dip dots
All Eyes are White with Black dip dots
Legs – Black
3. Sand the pieces and wipe clean.
4. Ink the outline details with the black marking pen.
5. Finish – Attach the bugs to the box with a cool temp glue gun. Brush Sparkle Glaze over the bug bodies.

TOP

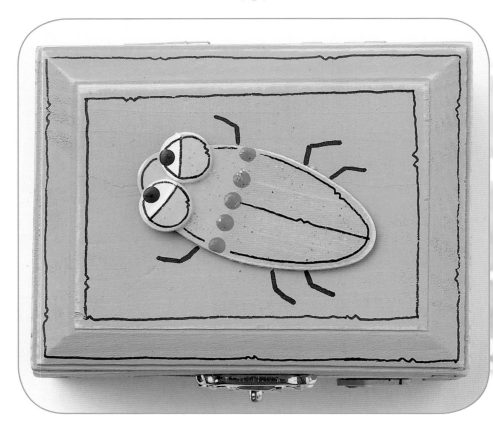

FRONT

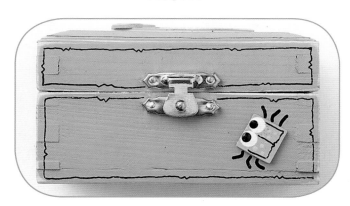

LEFT SIDE

RIGHT SIDE

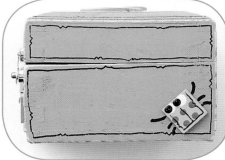

bug door hanger

Surface
3¹/₂" x 9¹/₂" Adoorable Hanger with Arch
(Lara's Crafts)
Wood Pieces
(2) Small Rectangles
(1) Medium Oval
(2) Small Ovals
(1) Small Triangle
(4) Small Circles
(1) Medium Square
(1) Small Square
Delta Ceramcoat® Medium
Sparkle Glaze
Delta Ceramcoat® Acrylic Paints
Tahiti Blue
White
Black
Green
Gecko
Citrus
OJ

INSTRUCTIONS
1. Assemble the bugs with Sobo® Glue.
2. Paint as follows:
Door Hanger – Tahiti Blue
Lettering – Black
Bug A – (1) Small Rectangle Citrus with
   Gecko dip dots
Bug B – (2) Small Circles and (1) Small Rectangle
   Citrus, (1) Small Triangle Gecko, (1) Medium
   Square Gecko with OJ dip dots
Bug C – (1) Small Square OJ with Citrus Stripes
Bug D – (1) Small Oval and (2) Small Circles
   Green, (1) Medium Oval Gecko with Green
   dip dots
Bug E – (1) Small Oval Gecko with OJ stripes
All Eyes – White with Black dip dots
3. Sand the pieces and wipe clean.
4. Ink the outline details with the black
   marking pen.
5. Finish – Attach the bugs to the door hanger
   with a cool temp glue gun. Brush Sparkle Glaze
   over the bug bodies.

train name plate

Surface
11¼" x 7¼" Wood Plaque

Wood Pieces
Wheels: (9) Medium Circles
(1) Large Circle
Engine: (1) Large Rectangle
(1) Large Square
(3) Small Squares
(1) Medium Triangle
(1) Mini Craft Stick
Cars: (1) Medium Square
(2) Large Squares
(1) XL Square
(1) Medium Star
(1) Large Circle
(1) Medium Heart

Other Supplies
Sawtooth Hanger

Delta Ceramcoat® Acrylic Paints
Blue Heaven
Opaque Red
OJ
Butter Yellow
Green
Opaque Blue
Black
White
Light Foliage Green
Medium Foliage Green

INSTRUCTIONS
1. Assemble the train engine with Sobo® Glue.
2. Attach a sawtooth hanger onto the back of the plaque.
3. Paint as follows:
Plaque – Blue Heaven
Engine – Opaque Red with White window
Mini Craft Stick – White
Engine Roof and Headlight – Butter Yellow
First train car – OJ with Green Circle
Second train car – Butter Yellow with Opaque Blue Heart
Third train car – Green with OJ Star
Fourth train car – Opaque Blue
Wheels and Words – Black
Grass Sprigs – Light Foliage Green and Medium Foliage Green
4. Sand the pieces and wipe clean. Sand heavily over the lettering.
5. Attach the star, heart and circle to the train cars using a cool temp glue gun.
6. Ink the outline details with the black marking pen.
7. Finish – Attach the engine and cars to the plaque using a cool temp glue gun.

train frame

Surface
5" x 5" Wood Photo Frame
Wood Pieces
Engine
(1) Medium Square
(1) Medium Rectangle
(3) Small Squares
(1) Small Triangle
(2) Small Circles
(1) Medium Circle
Cars
(2) Medium Squares
(4) Small Circles
(1) Small Heart
(1) Small Star
Wood Alphabet Tiles (desired letters)

Delta Ceramcoat® Acrylic Paints
Blue Heaven
Opaque Red
OJ
Butter Yellow
Green
Opaque Blue
Black
White

INSTRUCTIONS
1. Assemble the engine with Sobo® Glue.
2. Paint as follows:
Frame – Blue Heaven
Engine – Opaque Red with White window
Roof, Smokestack, and Headlight – Butter Yellow
First train car – Green with OJ Star
Second train car – Butter Yellow with Opaque Blue Heart
Wheels – Black
Alphabet Tiles – Butter Yellow wash
3. Sand the pieces and wipe clean.
4. Attach the star, heart, and wheels to the cars using a cool temp glue gun.
5. Ink the outline details with the black marking pen.
6. Finish – Attach the engine and cars to the frame with a cool temp glue gun. Attach the alphabet tiles to the top of the frame.

animals wall art

Surface
(3) 5" x 7" Stretched Canvases

Wood Pieces

Giraffe
(1) Medium Oval (Head)
(1) Large Oval (Body)
(1) Medium Star (Ears and Horns)
(5) Mini Craft Sticks (Neck, Legs)

Hippo
(1) XL Circle (Head)
(1) XXL Circle (Body)
(1) Large Oval (Nose)
(2) Small Squares (Teeth)
(2) Small Teardrops (Ears)
(4) Medium Teardrops (Feet)

Lion
(1) Large Circle (Head)
(2) Small Teardrops (Ears)
(2) XXL Circles (Mane and Body)
(5) Medium Teardrops (Feet and Tail)

Sun
(1) Medium Circle

Other Supplies
(3) Assorted Purple Buttons, Gold and Rust Craft Thread

Delta Ceramcoat® Acrylic Paints
Blue Heaven
Timberline Green
Light Foliage Green
Medium Foliage Green
Espresso
OJ
Butter Yellow
Black
Sweet Pea
White
Terra Cotta

INSTRUCTIONS:

1. Assemble the animals with Sobo® Glue.
2. Transfer the designs to the canvases.
3. Paint as follows:
Sky – Blue Heaven
Hills – Timberline Green; shade Medium Foliage Green and highlight Light Foliage Green
Grass and Palm Leaves – Medium Foliage Green, Light Foliage Green, and Espresso
Tree Trunks and Coconuts – Espresso
Flowers for Giraffe – OJ petals with Medium Foliage Green stems and leaves
Giraffe – Butter Yellow with Terra Cotta spots
Pond for Hippo – Blue Heaven
Hippo – Sweet Pea with OJ dots
Teeth – White
Lion and Sun – Butter Yellow
Lion's Mane – Butter Yellow with OJ
All Eyes and Noses – Black dip dots
4. Sand the pieces and wipe clean.
5. Ink the outline details with the black marking pen.
6. Attach the buttons to the flower centers with a cool temp glue gun.
7. Finish – Attach the animals and sun to the canvases with a cool temp glue gun. Holding both lengths together, tie the craft thread into a knot and glue to giraffe.

giraffe frame

Surface
5" x 5" Wood Photo Frame
Wood Pieces
Giraffe: (1) Small Star (ears and horns)
(2) Medium Ovals (head and neck)
(1) Large Circle (body)
(4) Mini Craft Sticks (legs)
Delta Ceramcoat® Acrylic Paints
Blue Heaven
Light Foliage Green
Green Tea
Medium Foliage Green

Espresso
Butter Yellow
OJ
Black

INSTRUCTIONS
1. Assemble the Giraffe with Sobo® Glue.
2. Paint as follows:
Frame – Blue Heaven
Hill and Grass – Light Foliage Green, highlight with Green Tea
Palm Trees – Medium Foliage Green leaves with Espresso trunks and coconuts

Grass Blades – Medium Foliage Green
Giraffe – OJ with Butter Yellow spots
Eyes – Black dip dots
3. Sand the pieces and wipe clean.
4. Ink the outline details with the black marking pen.
5. Finish – Attach the giraffe to the frame using a cool temp glue gun.

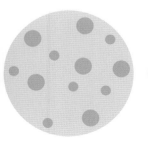
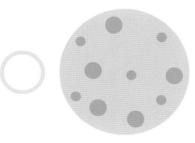
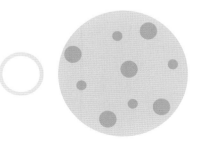
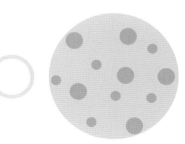

animal heads frame

Surface
5" x 5" Wood Photo Frame
Wood Pieces
Giraffe Head
(1) Medium Oval
(1) Small Star
Elephant Head
(1) Large Circle (head)
(2) Small Hearts (ears)
(1) Small Oval (trunk)
Lion Head
(1) XL Circle (mane)
(1) Large Circle (head)
(2) Small Circles (ears)
Hippo Head
(1) Large Circle (head)
(1) Medium Oval (nose)

(2) Small Circles (ears)
Delta Ceramcoat® Acrylic Paints
OJ
Butter Yellow
Black
Sweet Pea
Blissful Blue
Pink Frosting
Light Foliage Green

INSTRUCTIONS
1. Assemble the animal heads with Sobo® Glue.
2. Paint as follows:
Frame – Pink Frosting with Light Foliage Green dip dots
Giraffe Head – OJ with Butter

Yellow spots
Elephant Head – Blissful Blue with Butter Yellow dip dots
Lion Head – Butter Yellow with OJ mane
Hippo Head – Sweet Pea with OJ dip dots
Eyes and Noses – Black dip dots
3. Sand the pieces and wipe clean.
4. Ink the outline details with the black marking pen.
5. Finish – Attach the heads to the frame with a cool temp glue gun.

teapots wall art

Surface
(3) 3³/₄" Papier-mâché Circle Plaques
Wood Pieces
(3) XL Circles (teapots)
(3) Large Hearts (handles)
(3) Medium Teardrops (spouts)
(2) Medium Ovals (bases)
(1) Medium Triangle (base)
Delta Ceramcoat® Acrylic Paints
Pink Frosting
Hope
Think Pink
White
Sweet Pea
Blissful Blue
Light Foliage Green

INSTRUCTIONS
1. Assemble the Teapots with Sobo® Glue.
2. Paint as follows:
Plaques – Pink Frosting
Teapot A – Sweet Pea
Teapot B – Blissful Blue
Teapot C – Hope
Details on Teapot A – White
Details on Teapots B and C – Think Pink
Roses – Think Pink and White (Making Roses: Place one dip dot of Think Pink onto surface. Place one dip dot of White onto pink dip dot, just right of the center. Using a stylus or paintbrush handle, swirl these two colors together.)
Dip Dots around the edges of the plaques – Think Pink
Leaves – Light Foliage Green
3. Sand the pieces and wipe clean.
4. Ink the outline details with the black marking pen.
5. Finish – Attach the teapots to the plaques with a cool temp glue gun.

ballerina name plate

Surface
14" x 6" Innkeeper Signboard
(Walnut Hollow)
Wood Pieces
(1) Large Circle (Head)
(2) Small Stars (Hair)
(1) Large Star (Collar)
(1) Large Teardrop (Body)
(4) Medium Teardrops (Arms and Legs)
(1) Large Octagon (Skirt)
(2) XXL Ovals (ballet shoes)
Other Supplies
(2) 3" Twill Tape Strips, Sawtooth Hanger
Delta Ceramcoat® Medium
Sparkle Glaze
Delta Ceramcoat® Acrylic Paints
Green Tea
Peony

Pop Pink
Spice Tan
Think Pink
Fleshtone
Black
White

INSTRUCTIONS

1. Assemble the ballerina with Sobo® Glue.
2. Attach a sawtooth hanger to the back of the sign.
3. Paint as follows:
Sign – Green Tea
Shoes – Peony inside and Pop Pink outside
Ballerina arms, legs, and face – Fleshtone
Hair – Spice Tan

Leotard – Pop Pink
Collar and Skirt – Think Pink with White dip dots
Eyes – Black dip dots
Lettering – Pop Pink
4. Sand the pieces and wipe clean.
5. Ink the outline details with the black marking pen.
6. Finish – Attach the ballerina and shoes to the sign using a cool temp glue gun. Knot the twill tape to create two bows. Attach the bows to the ballet shoes. Trim twill tape ends. Brush Sparkle Glaze over the leotard.

ballet shoes peg rack

Surface
1½" x 11⅞" Wood Peg Rack
Wood Pieces
(6) Medium Ovals (shoes)
(2) Medium Circles (heads)
(2) Small Circles (hair buns)
Other Supplies
(3) Small Bows, Sawtooth
Hanger, Pink Powder Blush
**Delta Ceramcoat® Acrylic
Paints**
Green Tea
Pop Pink
Spice Tan
Think Pink
Fleshtone
Black
Blissful Blue
Blue Heaven

Enchanted
Sweet Pea
Straw

INSTRUCTIONS
1. Assemble the ballerina
   heads with Sobo® Glue.
2. Paint as follows:
Peg Rack – Green Tea
1st Pair of Shoes – Sweet Pea
   with Enchanted inside
2nd Pair of Shoes – Pop Pink
   with Think Pink inside
3rd Pair of Shoes – Blue
   Heaven with Blissful Blue
   inside
Ballerina A – Fleshtone with
   Spice Tan hair

Ballerina B – Fleshtone with
   Straw hair
Eyes – Black dip dots
3. Blush the cheeks using pink
   powder blush.
4. Sand the pieces and wipe
   clean.
5. Ink the outline details with
   the black marking pen.
6. Attach the pieces to the rack
   with a cool temp glue gun.
7. Finish – Attach the bows to
   the heels of the ballet shoes
   with a cool temp glue gun.
   Attach a sawtooth hanger to
   the back of the peg rack.

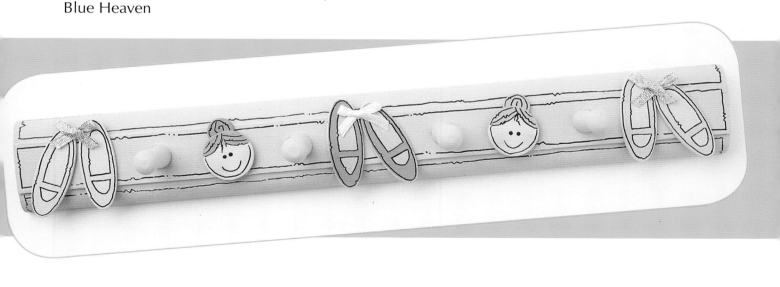

cow sign

Surface
Forster® Woodsies®
7¼" x 2¹³/₁₆" x ¼" Wood Slat

Wood Pieces
Cow Head
(1) XL Oval (head)
(1) Large Octagon (nose)
(1) XL Star (ears, horns)
Cow
(1) Large Square (body)
(1) Small Rectangle (head)
(1) Medium Circle (nose)
(1) Small Star (ears, horns)
(2) Small Teardrops (feet)
(1) Small Oval (tail)

Other Supplies
(2) Small Screw Eyes, Needle Nose Pliers, 12" Ribbon for hanging, Ribbon Scraps for rag bows

Delta Ceramcoat® Acrylic Paints
White
Black
Pink Frosting
Blissful Blue

INSTRUCTIONS:
1. Assemble the cow and cow head with Sobo® Glue.
2. Paint as follows:
Slat – White with Blissful Blue spots
Lettering – Black
Cows – White with Black spots and dip dot eyes
Noses – Pink Frosting with Black dip dot nostrils
3. Sand the pieces and wipe clean. Sand heavily over the lettering.

4. Ink the outline details with the black marking pen.
5. Attach the cow and cow head to the sign using a cool temp glue gun.
6. Finish – Press and twist the screw eyes into the top of the sign. Use the pliers to tighten. Thread the long ribbon through the screw eyes; knot the ribbon ends. Knot the ribbon scraps and attach to cows' necks with cool temp glue gun. Trim the ribbon ends.

cow plant poke

Surface
Jumbo Craft Stick
Wood Pieces
(1) XL Square (body)
(1) Medium Oval (head)
(1) Medium Circle (nose)
(1) Small Star (ears and horns)
(2) Small Rectangles (feet)
(1) Small Oval (tail)
Other Supplies
3" ribbon scrap for rag bow
Delta Ceramcoat® Acrylic Paints
White
Black
Pink Frosting
Moroccan Red

INSTRUCTIONS
1. Assemble the cow with Sobo® Glue.
2. Paint as follows:
Jumbo Craft Stick – Moroccan Red
Cow – White with Black spots and dip dot eyes
Nose – Pink Frosting with Black dip dot nostrils
3. Sand the pieces and wipe clean.
4. Ink the outline details with the black marking pen.
5. Finish – Attach the cow to the craft stick using a cool temp glue gun. Knot the center of the ribbon and attach using a cool temp glue gun.

cow magnet

Wood Pieces
(1) XXL Square (body)
(3) Medium Rectangles (head, feet)
(1) Medium Octagon (nose)
(1) Large Star (ears, horns)
(1) Medium Oval (tail)
Other Supplies
Round Button Magnet, 4" Ribbon Scrap for rag bow
Delta Ceramcoat® Acrylic Paints
White
Black
Pink Frosting

INSTRUCTIONS
1. Assemble the cow with Sobo® Glue.
2. Paint as follows:
Cow – White with Black spots and dip dot eyes
Nose – Pink Frosting with Black dip dot nostrils
3. Sand the pieces and wipe clean.
4. Ink the outline details with the black marking pen.
5. Finish – Attach the button magnet to the back of the cow using a cool temp glue gun. Knot the ribbon and attach using a cool temp glue gun. Trim ribbon ends.

chicken sign

Surface
Forster® Woodsies®
7¹/₄" x 2¹³/₁₆" x ¹/₄" Wood Slat
Wood Pieces
Chicken:
(1) XL Oval (body)
(2) Small Stars (wings)
(2) Medium Stars (comb)
(1) Small Triangle (beak)
Chicken Head:
(1) XL Oval (head)
(1) XL Star (comb)
(1) Small Triangle (beak)
Other Supplies
(2) Small Screw Eyes, Needle
Nose Pliers, 12" fabric strip for
hanger, 3" coordinating fabric
strip
**Delta Ceramcoat® Acrylic
Paints**
White
Black

Blissful Blue
Moroccan Red
Citrus

INSTRUCTIONS:
1. Assemble the chickens with
   Sobo® Glue. (Note: for the
   smaller comb, glue two stars
   back-to-back for stability).
2. Paint as follows:
Slat – White with Blissful Blue
   spots
Lettering – Black
Chicken – Black with White
   dots
Eyes – Large White dip dots
   with smaller Black dip dot
   centers
Chicken Head – White
Eyes – Black dip dots
Combs – Moroccan Red
Beaks – Citrus

3. Sand the pieces and wipe
   clean. Sand heavily over the
   lettering.
4. Ink the outline details with
   the black marking pen.
5. Attach the chicken and
   chicken head to the sign
   using a cool temp glue gun.
6. Finish – Press and twist the
   screw eyes into the top of
   the sign. Use the pliers to
   tighten. Thread the long
   fabric strip through the
   screw eyes; knot the fabric
   ends. Knot the short fabric
   strip to the center of the
   hanger. Trim the fabric ends.

chicken plant poke

Surface
Jumbo Craft Stick
Wood Pieces
(1) XL Oval (body)
(2) Small Stars (wings)
(2) Medium Stars (comb)
(1) Small Triangle (beak)
Delta Ceramcoat® Acrylic Paints
White
Black
Moroccan Red
Citrus

INSTRUCTIONS
1. Assemble the chicken with Sobo® Glue. (Note: for the comb, glue two stars back-to-back for stability).
2. Paint as follows:
Jumbo Craft Stick – Moroccan Red
Chicken – White with Black dip dots
Eyes – Black dip dots
Beak – Citrus
Comb – Moroccan Red
3. Sand the pieces and wipe clean.
4. Ink the outline details with the black marking pen.
5. Finish – Attach the chicken to the craft stick using a cool temp glue gun.

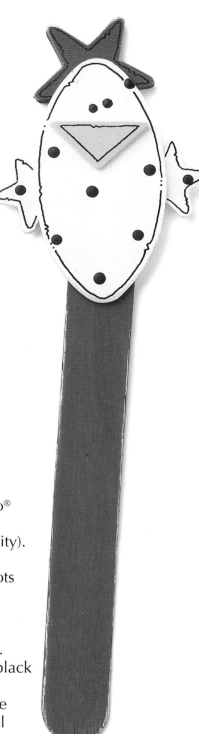

chicken magnet

Wood Pieces
(1) XXL Oval (body)
(2) Medium Stars (wings)
(2) Large Stars (comb)
(1) Medium Triangle (beak)
Other Supplies
Round Button Magnet
Delta Ceramcoat® Acrylic Paints
White
Black
Moroccan Red
Citrus

INSTRUCTIONS
1. Assemble the chicken with Sobo® Glue. (Note: for the comb, glue two stars back-to-back for stability).
2. Paint as follows:
Chicken – White with Black dip dots
Eyes – Black dip dots
Beak – Citrus
Comb – Moroccan Red
3. Sand the pieces and wipe clean.
4. Ink the outline details with the black marking pen.
5. Finish – Attach the magnet to the back of the chicken using a cool temp glue gun.

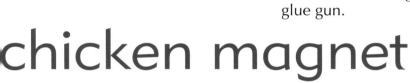

pig sign

Surface
Forster® Woodsies®
7¼" x 2¹³/₁₆" x ¼" Wood Slat
Wood Pieces
Pig Head
(1) XL Circle (head)
(1) Medium Oval (nose),
(2) Medium Triangles (ears)
Pig
(1) XL Circle (body)
(1) Large Circle (head)
(1) Small Oval (nose)
(2) Small Triangles (ears)
(2) Small Octagons (feet)
Other Supplies
(2) Small Screw Eyes, 12"
length Ribbon for hanging,
Ribbon Scrap for rag bow,
3" length Pink Rickrack

Delta Ceramcoat® Acrylic Paints
White
Black
Blissful Blue
Pink Frosting
Think Pink

INSTRUCTIONS:
1. Assemble the pig and pig head with Sobo® Glue.
2. Paint as follows:
Slat – White with Blissful Blue dip dots
Lettering – Black
Pig Heads, Ears, and Feet – Pink Frosting
Pig Body – Pink Frosting with Think Pink dip dots
Eyes – Black dip dots
Nostrils and Feet – Black

3. Sand the pieces and wipe clean. Sand heavily over the lettering.
4. Ink the outline details with the black marking pen.
5. Attach the pig and pig head to the sign using a cool temp glue gun.
6. Finish – Press and twist the screw eyes into the top of the sign. Use the pliers to tighten. Thread the long ribbon through the screw eyes; knot the ribbon ends. Knot the short ribbon piece. Attach the knotted ribbon and folded rickrack to the sign. Trim the ribbon ends.

pig plant poke

Surface
Jumbo Craft Stick

Wood Pieces
Pig: (1) XXL Circle (body)
(1) XL Circle (head)
(1) Medium Oval (nose)
(2) Small Hearts (ears)
(2) Medium Hearts (feet)

Other Supplies
White Satin Bow, 3" length of Pink Rickrack

Delta Ceramcoat® Acrylic Paints
White
Black
Think Pink
Moroccan Red

INSTRUCTIONS
1. Assemble the pig with Sobo® Glue.
2. Paint as follows:
Jumbo Craft Stick – Moroccan Red
Pig – Think Pink with White dip dots
Eyes – Black dip dots
Nostrils and Feet – Black
3. Sand the pieces and wipe clean.
4. Ink the outline details with the black marking pen.
5. Finish – Attach the pig to the craft stick with a cool temp glue gun. Attach the bow and rickrack tail using a cool temp glue gun.

sheep sign

Surface
Forster® Woodsies®
7¼" x 2¹³⁄₁₆" x ¼" Wood Slat
Wood Pieces
Sheep
(1) XL Circle (body)
(1) Large Oval (head)
(2) Small Teardrops (ears)
(4) Medium Ovals (feet)
(1) Small Oval (tail)
Sheep Head
(1) XL Oval (head)
(1) Large Star (wool)
(2) Medium Ovals (ears)
Other Supplies
(2) Small Screw Eyes, Needle
Nose Pliers, 12" Fabric Strip,
3" Coordinating Fabric Strip,
Ribbon for Rag Bow

Delta Ceramcoat® Acrylic Paints:
White
Black

INSTRUCTIONS:
1. Assemble the sheep and sheep
   head with Sobo® Glue.
2. Paint as follows:
Slat – White
Lettering – Black
Sheep Body – White
Sheep Heads, Ears and Feet –
   Black
Sheep Head Wool and Noses –
   White
Eyes – Large White dip dots with
   smaller Black dip dot centers
3. Sand the pieces and wipe
   clean. Sand heavily over the
   lettering.

4. Ink the outline details with the
   black marking pen.
5. Attach the sheep and sheep
   head to the sign using a cool
   temp glue gun.
6. Finish – Press and twist the
   screw eyes into the top of the
   sign. Use the pliers to tighten.
   Thread the long fabric strip
   through the screw eyes; knot
   the fabric ends. Knot the short
   fabric strip to the center of the
   hanger. Knot the ribbon and
   attach to the sheep. Trim the
   fabric and ribbon ends.

sheep door hanger

Surface
$3^{1}/_{2}$" x $9^{1}/_{2}$" Adoorable Hanger with Arch, $2^{1}/_{2}$" Wood Fence (Lara's Crafts)

Wood Pieces
(1) Medium Octagon (body)
(1) Medium Oval (head)
(2) Small Teardrops (ears)
(4) Small Ovals (feet)
(1) Small Circle (tail)

Delta Ceramcoat® Acrylic Paints
White
Black
Blissful Blue
Blue Heaven

INSTRUCTIONS
1. Assemble the sheep with Sobo® Glue.
2. Paint as follows:
Door Hanger – Base coat Blue Heaven. Sponge over with Blissful Blue
Fence – White
Sheep Body, Tail – White
Sheep Head, Ears, and Feet – Black
Eyes – White dip dots with smaller Black dip dot centers
Nose – White
3. Sand the pieces and wipe clean.
4. Ink the outline details with the black marking pen.
5. Finish – Attach the fence and sheep to the door hanger using a cool temp glue gun.

sheep magnet

Wood Pieces
(1) XXL Circle (body)
(1) Large Oval (head)
(2) Small Teardrops (ears)
(4) Mini Craft Sticks (feet)
(1) Small Oval (tail)

Other Supplies
Round Button Magnet, Red Satin Bow

Delta Ceramcoat® Acrylic Paints
White
Black

INSTRUCTIONS:
1. Assemble the Sheep with Sobo® Glue.
2. Paint as follows:
Body and Tail – White
Head, Ears and Feet – Black
Nose – White
Eyes – Large White dip dots with smaller Black dip dot centers.
3. Sand the pieces and wipe clean.
4. Ink the outline details with the black marking pen.
5. Finish – Attach the magnet to the back of the sheep with a cool temp glue gun. Attach the satin bow with a cool temp glue gun.

paint conversion chart

Delta Ceramcoat®	DecoArt™ Americana	Plaid® FolkArt®
Barn Red	Deep Burgundy	True Burgundy (AP)
Black	Black (Ebony/Lamp)	Licorice
Blissful Blue	Winter Blue	Baby Blue
Blue Heaven	Baby Blue	Light Blue
Butter Yellow	True Ochre + White	Turner's Yellow (AP)
Citrus	Yellow Light	Yellow Light (AP)
Dark Foliage Green	Hauser Green Dark + Deep Teal	Hauser Green Dark (AP)
Drizzle Grey	Dove Grey + Sky Grey	Light Grey + Porcelain Blue
Enchanted		
Espresso	Asphaltum + Fawn	
Fleshtone	Flesh Tone	Georgia Peach + Skintone
Gecko		
Golden Brown	Honey Brown	English Mustard
Green		
Green Tea	Jade Green + Taffy Cream	Ice Green Light + Bayberry
Hope		
Laguna Blue	Desert Turquoise + Bluegrass Green	Aqua (AP)
Latte	Camel	Cappuccino
Light Foliage Green	Hauser Light Green	Hauser Light Green (AP)
Mediterranean	Snow White + True Blue + Ultra Blue Deep	
Medium Foliage Green	Hauser Medium Green	Hauser Medium Green (AP)
Moroccan Red	Crimson Tide	Barnyard Red
OJ		
Opaque Blue	Ultramarine Blue	Brilliant Blue
Opaque Red	Calico Red	Christmas Red + Red Light
Peony	Pink Chiffon + Snow White	Portrait Light
Pink Frosting	Hi-Lite Flesh	White + Sweetheart Pink
Pop Pink	Bubble Gum Pink	Pink
Spa Blue	Soft Lilac	Hydrangea
Spice Brown	Milk Chocolate	Nutmeg
Spice Tan	Antique Gold + Sable Brown	Honeycomb
Straw	Golden Straw	Buttercup
Sweet Pea		
Tahiti Blue	Desert Turquoise	Aqua (AP)
Terra Cotta	Terra Cotta + Burnt Orange	Glazed Carrots + English Mustard
Think Pink	Poodleskirt Pink	Baby Pink
Timberline Green	Plantation Pine + Pumpkin	Olive Green + Teddy Bear Tan
White	White (Snow or Titanium)	White (Titanium) (AP)

(AP) FolkArt® Artists' Pigments™